This Movie Log Book belongs to:

_____

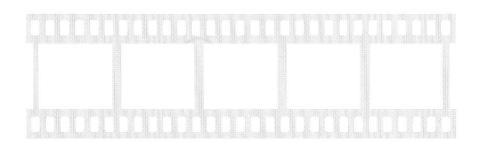

My Movie Log Book

Movie Title:

Director:

Genre:

Setting (*Time and Place*):

Main Cast:

Supporting Cast:

Plot:

My Movie Log Book

My Review:

_____

_____

_____

_____

_____

_____

_____

_____

_____

Extra notes:

_____

_____

_____

Movie Rating: ☆☆☆☆☆

My Movie Log Book

Movie Title:

Director:

Genre:

Setting (*Time and Place*):

Main Cast:

Supporting Cast:

Plot:

My Movie Log Book

My Review:

Extra notes:

Movie Rating: ☆☆☆☆☆

My Movie Log Book

Movie Title:

Director:

Genre:

Setting (*Time and Place*):

Main Cast:

Supporting Cast:

Plot:

My Movie Log Book

My Review:

_____

_____

_____

_____

_____

_____

_____

_____

Extra notes:

_____

_____

_____

Movie Rating: ☆☆☆☆☆

My Movie Log Book

Movie Title:

Director:

Genre:

Setting (*Time and Place*):

Main Cast:

Supporting Cast:

Plot:

My Movie Log Book

My Review:

Extra notes:

Movie Rating: ☆☆☆☆☆

My Movie Log Book

Movie Title:

Director:

Genre:

Setting (*Time and Place*):

Main Cast:

Supporting Cast:

Plot:

My Movie Log Book

My Review:

_____

_____

_____

_____

_____

_____

_____

Extra notes:

_____

_____

_____

Movie Rating: ☆☆☆☆☆

My Movie Log Book

Movie Title:

Director:

Genre:

Setting (*Time and Place*):

Main Cast:

Supporting Cast:

Plot:

My Movie Log Book

My Review:

Extra notes:

Movie Rating: ☆☆☆☆☆

My Movie Log Book

Movie Title:

Director:

Genre:

Setting (*Time and Place*):

Main Cast:

Supporting Cast:

Plot:

My Movie Log Book

My Review:

_____

_____

_____

_____

_____

_____

_____

_____

Extra notes:

_____

_____

_____

Movie Rating: ☆☆☆☆☆

My Movie Log Book

Movie Title:

Director:

Genre:

Setting (*Time and Place*):

Main Cast:

Supporting Cast:

Plot:

My Movie Log Book

My Review:

_____

_____

_____

_____

_____

_____

_____

Extra notes:

_____

_____

_____

Movie Rating: ☆☆☆☆☆

My Movie Log Book

Movie Title:

Director:

Genre:

Setting (*Time and Place*):

Main Cast:

Supporting Cast:

Plot:

My Movie Log Book

My Review:

_____

_____

_____

_____

_____

_____

_____

_____

_____

Extra notes:

_____

_____

_____

Movie Rating: ☆ ☆ ☆ ☆ ☆

My Movie Log Book

Movie Title:

Director:

Genre:

Setting (*Time and Place*):

Main Cast:

Supporting Cast:

Plot:

My Movie Log Book

My Review:

Extra notes:

Movie Rating: ☆☆☆☆☆

My Movie Log Book

Movie Title:

Director:

Genre:

Setting (*Time and Place*):

Main Cast:

Supporting Cast:

Plot:

My Movie Log Book

My Review:

Extra notes:

Movie Rating: ☆☆☆☆☆

My Movie Log Book

Movie Title:

Director:

Genre:

Setting (*Time and Place*):

Main Cast:

Supporting Cast:

Plot:

My Movie Log Book

My Review:

_____

_____

_____

_____

_____

_____

_____

_____

_____

_____

Extra notes:

_____

_____

_____

Movie Rating: ☆☆☆☆☆

My Movie Log Book

Movie Title:

Director:

Genre:

Setting (*Time and Place*):

Main Cast:

Supporting Cast:

Plot:

My Movie Log Book

My Review:

Extra notes:

Movie Rating: ☆☆☆☆☆

My Movie Log Book

Movie Title:

Director:

Genre:

Setting (*Time and Place*):

Main Cast:

Supporting Cast:

Plot:

My Movie Log Book

My Review:

_____

_____

_____

_____

_____

_____

_____

_____

Extra notes:

_____

_____

_____

Movie Rating: ☆☆☆☆☆

My Movie Log Book

Movie Title:

Director:

Genre:

Setting (*Time and Place*):

Main Cast:

Supporting Cast:

Plot:

My Movie Log Book

My Review:

Extra notes:

Movie Rating: ☆☆☆☆☆

My Movie Log Book

Movie Title:

Director:

Genre:

Setting (*Time and Place*):

Main Cast:

Supporting Cast:

Plot:

My Movie Log Book

My Review:

_____

_____

_____

_____

_____

_____

_____

_____

_____

Extra notes:

_____

_____

_____

Movie Rating: ☆☆☆☆☆

My Movie Log Book

Movie Title:

Director:

Genre:

Setting (*Time and Place*):

Main Cast:

Supporting Cast:

Plot:

My Movie Log Book

My Review:

Extra notes:

Movie Rating: ☆☆☆☆☆

My Movie Log Book

Movie Title:

Director:

Genre:

Setting (*Time and Place*):

Main Cast:

Supporting Cast:

Plot:

My Movie Log Book

My Review:

_____

_____

_____

_____

_____

_____

_____

_____

Extra notes:

_____

_____

_____

Movie Rating: ☆☆☆☆☆

My Movie Log Book

Movie Title:

Director:

Genre:

Setting (*Time and Place*):

Main Cast:

Supporting Cast:

Plot:

My Movie Log Book

My Review:

_____

_____

_____

_____

_____

_____

_____

_____

Extra notes:

_____

_____

_____

Movie Rating: ☆ ☆ ☆ ☆ ☆

My Movie Log Book

Movie Title:

Director:

Genre:

Setting (*Time and Place*):

Main Cast:

Supporting Cast:

Plot:

My Movie Log Book

My Review:

Extra notes:

Movie Rating: ☆☆☆☆☆

My Movie Log Book

Movie Title:

Director:

Genre:

Setting (*Time and Place*):

Main Cast:

Supporting Cast:

Plot:

My Movie Log Book

My Review:

_____

_____

_____

_____

_____

_____

_____

_____

_____

Extra notes:

_____

_____

_____

Movie Rating: ☆☆☆☆☆

My Movie Log Book

Movie Title:

Director:

Genre:

Setting (*Time and Place*):

Main Cast:

Supporting Cast:

Plot:

My Movie Log Book

My Review:

_____

_____

_____

_____

_____

_____

_____

_____

_____

Extra notes:

_____

_____

_____

Movie Rating: ☆☆☆☆☆

My Movie Log Book

Movie Title:

Director:

Genre:

Setting (*Time and Place*):

Main Cast:

Supporting Cast:

Plot:

My Movie Log Book

My Review:

_____

_____

_____

_____

_____

_____

_____

_____

_____

Extra notes:

_____

_____

_____

Movie Rating: ☆☆☆☆☆

My Movie Log Book

Movie Title:

Director:

Genre:

Setting (*Time and Place*):

Main Cast:

Supporting Cast:

Plot:

My Movie Log Book

My Review:

Extra notes:

Movie Rating: ☆☆☆☆☆

My Movie Log Book

Movie Title:

Director:

Genre:

Setting (*Time and Place*):

Main Cast:

Supporting Cast:

Plot:

My Movie Log Book

My Review:

Extra notes:

Movie Rating: ☆☆☆☆☆

My Movie Log Book

Movie Title:

Director:

Genre:

Setting (*Time and Place*):

Main Cast:

Supporting Cast:

Plot:

My Movie Log Book

My Review:

Extra notes:

Movie Rating: ☆☆☆☆☆

My Movie Log Book

Movie Title:

Director:

Genre:

Setting (*Time and Place*):

Main Cast:

Supporting Cast:

Plot:

My Movie Log Book

My Review:

_____

_____

_____

_____

_____

_____

_____

_____

Extra notes:

_____

_____

_____

_____

Movie Rating: ☆☆☆☆☆

My Movie Log Book

Movie Title:

Director:

Genre:

Setting (*Time and Place*):

Main Cast:

Supporting Cast:

Plot:

My Movie Log Book

My Review:

_____

_____

_____

_____

_____

_____

_____

Extra notes:

_____

_____

_____

Movie Rating: ☆☆☆☆☆

My Movie Log Book

Movie Title:

Director:

Genre:

Setting (*Time and Place*):

Main Cast:

Supporting Cast:

Plot:

My Movie Log Book

My Review:

Extra notes:

Movie Rating: ☆☆☆☆☆

My Movie Log Book

Movie Title:

Director:

Genre:

Setting (*Time and Place*):

Main Cast:

Supporting Cast:

Plot:

My Movie Log Book

My Review:

Extra notes:

Movie Rating: ☆☆☆☆☆

My Movie Log Book

Movie Title:

Director:

Genre:

Setting (*Time and Place*):

Main Cast:

Supporting Cast:

Plot:

My Movie Log Book

My Review:

Extra notes:

Movie Rating: ☆☆☆☆☆

My Movie Log Book

Movie Title:

Director:

Genre:

Setting (*Time and Place*):

Main Cast:

Supporting Cast:

Plot:

My Movie Log Book

My Review:

_____

_____

_____

_____

_____

_____

_____

_____

Extra notes:

_____

_____

_____

Movie Rating: ☆☆☆☆☆

My Movie Log Book

Movie Title:

Director:

Genre:

Setting (*Time and Place*):

Main Cast:

Supporting Cast:

Plot:

My Movie Log Book

My Review:

Extra notes:

Movie Rating: ☆☆☆☆☆

My Movie Log Book

Movie Title:

Director:

Genre:

Setting (*Time and Place*):

Main Cast:

Supporting Cast:

Plot:

My Movie Log Book

My Review:

_____

_____

_____

_____

_____

_____

_____

_____

Extra notes:

_____

_____

_____

Movie Rating: ☆ ☆ ☆ ☆ ☆

My Movie Log Book

Movie Title:

Director:

Genre:

Setting (*Time and Place*):

Main Cast:

Supporting Cast:

Plot:

My Movie Log Book

My Review:

Extra notes:

Movie Rating: ☆☆☆☆☆

My Movie Log Book

Movie Title:

Director:

Genre:

Setting (*Time and Place*):

Main Cast:

Supporting Cast:

Plot:

My Movie Log Book

My Review:

_____

_____

_____

_____

_____

_____

_____

Extra notes:

_____

_____

_____

Movie Rating: ☆ ☆ ☆ ☆ ☆

My Movie Log Book

Movie Title:

Director:

Genre:

Setting (*Time and Place*):

Main Cast:

Supporting Cast:

Plot:

My Movie Log Book

My Review:

_____

_____

_____

_____

_____

_____

_____

Extra notes:

_____

_____

_____

Movie Rating:

My Movie Log Book

Movie Title:

Director:

Genre:

Setting (*Time and Place*):

Main Cast:

Supporting Cast:

Plot:

My Movie Log Book

My Review:

Extra notes:

Movie Rating: ☆☆☆☆☆

My Movie Log Book

Movie Title:

Director:

Genre:

Setting (Time and Place):

Main Cast:

Supporting Cast:

Plot:

My Movie Log Book

My Review:

_____

_____

_____

_____

_____

_____

_____

_____

_____

Extra notes:

_____

_____

_____

_____

Movie Rating: ☆☆☆☆☆

My Movie Log Book

Movie Title:

Director:

Genre:

Setting (*Time and Place*):

Main Cast:

Supporting Cast:

Plot:

My Movie Log Book

My Review:

Extra notes:

Movie Rating:

My Movie Log Book

Movie Title:

Director:

Genre:

Setting (*Time and Place*):

Main Cast:

Supporting Cast:

Plot:

My Movie Log Book

My Review:

_____

_____

_____

_____

_____

_____

_____

_____

Extra notes:

_____

_____

_____

Movie Rating: ☆☆☆☆☆

My Movie Log Book

Movie Title:

Director:

Genre:

Setting (Time and Place):

Main Cast:

Supporting Cast:

Plot:

My Movie Log Book

My Review:

_____

_____

_____

_____

_____

_____

_____

Extra notes:

_____

_____

_____

Movie Rating: ☆☆☆☆☆

My Movie Log Book

Movie Title:

Director:

Genre:

Setting (*Time and Place*):

Main Cast:

Supporting Cast:

Plot:

My Movie Log Book

My Review:

Extra notes:

Movie Rating: ☆☆☆☆☆

My Movie Log Book

Movie Title:

Director:

Genre:

Setting (*Time and Place*):

Main Cast:

Supporting Cast:

Plot:

My Movie Log Book

My Review:

Extra notes:

Movie Rating: ☆☆☆☆☆

My Movie Log Book

Movie Title:

Director:

Genre:

Setting (*Time and Place*):

Main Cast:

Supporting Cast:

Plot:

My Movie Log Book

My Review:

Extra notes:

Movie Rating: ☆☆☆☆☆

My Movie Log Book

Movie Title:

Director:

Genre:

Setting (*Time and Place*):

Main Cast:

Supporting Cast:

Plot:

My Movie Log Book

My Review:

_____

_____

_____

_____

_____

_____

_____

_____

_____

Extra notes:

_____

_____

_____

Movie Rating: ☆☆☆☆☆

My Movie Log Book

Movie Title:

Director:

Genre:

Setting (*Time and Place*):

Main Cast:

Supporting Cast:

Plot:

My Movie Log Book

My Review:

_____

_____

_____

_____

_____

_____

_____

_____

Extra notes:

_____

_____

_____

Movie Rating: ☆☆☆☆☆

My Movie Log Book

Movie Title:

Director:

Genre:

Setting (*Time and Place*):

Main Cast:

Supporting Cast:

Plot:

My Movie Log Book

My Review:

_____

_____

_____

_____

_____

_____

_____

_____

Extra notes:

_____

_____

_____

Movie Rating: ☆☆☆☆☆

My Movie Log Book

Movie Title:

Director:

Genre:

Setting (Time and Place):

Main Cast:

Supporting Cast:

Plot:

My Movie Log Book

My Review:

Extra notes:

Movie Rating: ☆☆☆☆☆

My Movie Log Book

Movie Title:

Director:

Genre:

Setting (*Time and Place*):

Main Cast:

Supporting Cast:

Plot:

My Movie Log Book

My Review:

_____

_____

_____

_____

_____

_____

_____

_____

_____

Extra notes:

_____

_____

_____

Movie Rating: ☆☆☆☆☆

Made in United States
Orlando, FL
15 November 2021